East Cosham

The first part of our latest booklet covers part of th[illegible]a Island known as Cosham, covering from th[illegible] but, not including Drayton Lane, from t[illegible]tsdown Hill.

The Highbury Estate, Wymering [illegible]earlier booklets, also covered in a separa[illegible]

Historical Background

The Cosham to Chichester Turnpike was formed in 1762. They purchased a strip of the common field and formed a by-pass from Mulberry Lane to Park Lane which effectively split the common field in two. Park Lane the original route of the main road plunged hazardously down to the south. Park Lane was formerly known as Upper Park Road and Water Lane, an old map shows conduits at the bottom, presumably it was very wet taking the water which ran down the hill.

The East Court Estate was developed in 1923/4 by D Gammans with bungalows and houses built by A.J Chase, M.G Coleman, G.H Nicholls and others. The East Court Trust, with solicitor H.M Gammans, was still in existence in 1954 when they gave up land for the widening of Court Lane.
In 1924 the grounds of the Cosham House Estate were laid out for building with two 40 foot roads leading north.

Cosham Hutments was an area of dwellings on small plots that stood on the south side of London Road down to where Southdown Road is now and between Widley Road and East Cosham Road. The original huts were wooden. In 1919 questions were asked in Parliament as to why the Non-Combatant Corps had not been demobilised. Later they could have been added to by more modern pre-fabs. By 1933, there were 26 dwellings and by 1951 there were 70 dwellings.
In 1933 a family moved into the army officers huts halfway down Portsdown Hill. They used to see the Army Band marching back from Church Parade at St Colman's Church.
Andrea Coleman via Facebook commented that her father was an army officer and they lived there before WW2 but left in 1944 after he was killed and they went to live with her grandmother.
Council Minutes in 1951 refer to Bungalow Hut No 8, Cosham Hutments, London Road. In 1952 a Compulsory Purchase Order was issued for occupied

hutments, 1, 1a, 2-8 inclusive and sites of the other hutments. Also in 1955 part of Widley Road from the London Road down to the hutments was stopped up when Widley Road was widened.

> "We lived in one of the huts when I was around 4 years old. We lived in the Hutments because my father was an NCO in the Royal Army Ordnance Corps and they were Army quarters. I remember they were cold, long and narrow with a wooden floor that made a lovely noise when I jumped up and down. I was always being told to stop jumping on the floor. There were steps at the front that my brother and I used to sit on around which my mother planted flowers. I also remember that we all used to run down the hill to go to school. I do not remember us having a bathroom but the toilet used to empty into a tub under the hut as they were on stilts and somebody would empty the tub but I can't remember who."
>
> Patricia Cleal

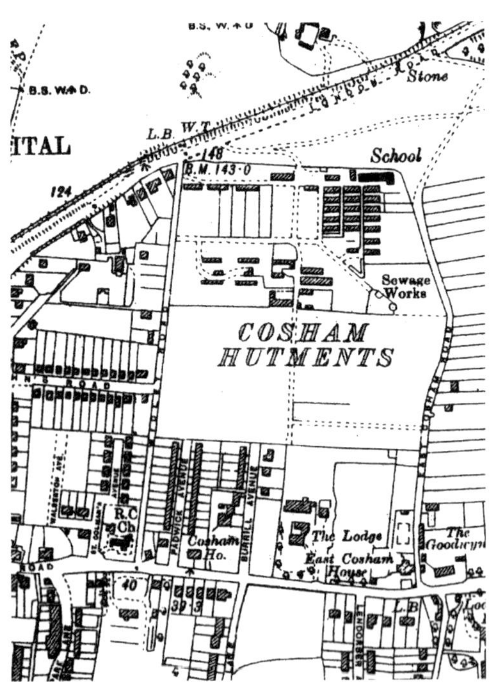

Extract from 1932 Ordnance Survey Map

General Memories

"After Pamela Boothby's wedding to Claude at St Andrews Church, Farlington, and the reception at the Sandringham Hotel in Southsea we all adjourned to her parents bungalow in Court Mead for more refreshments. The bungalow took a lot of space and had a large garden, we were regularly shown around the garden to see the latest developments, new plants etc. At the front of the bungalow was a walled garden with a lawned area and Mrs New, who as Miss Smith delivered milk in churns to the midnight milkman at Green Farm, had a stone cat and stone tortoise there. Brian , Pamela's new brother-in-law said he had spent five minutes filming the tortoise. The star turn at the bungalow was Pam's grandfather who had worked in the Co-operative Dairy in Drayton. He died a few week's after this unfortunately. After this reception Mary and Bryan Miller, Dave Webb and I, Ernest and Valerie New, Brian Boothby and his wife, went to the Red Lion, Cosham. Talk about changes of scene. One of the interests at the Red Lion was the milestone at the rear.
I sent away for a sewing kit which I had got from a woman's magazine. It consisted of a Pakistani style blue-black and slightly off white long sleeved tunic, off white flared trousers and a matching scarf that needed putting together. I saw an advertisement, a dressmaker's telephone number on the notice board outside the News shop which had Brian's of London hairdresser's above it where my cousin Ann worked with her friend. René Prandy, my friend Pat's mum, worked in the Newsagents. I saw the advertisement because the buses used to stop outside probably where Boots the chemists now is. Dave loaned me the Ford Cortina car and I went for a fitting to Burrill Avenue. The house was very oldie worldly inside with dark brown wood panelling. It had a downstairs laundry and ironing room which I was impressed by. On the way back I was on the Eastern Road when the water pump went on the car. I couldn't even open the bonnet, so had to flag down passing motorists, one stopped and he turned out to be a mechanic, he was with a woman and a man, they towed the car to outside my house in Hilsea and said they'd come back the following evening to repair it. I had to go down by bus to the Savoy Cinema in Commercial Road to collect Dave my husband. I didn''t live this down easily."

Sylvia Webb

Street List

The following listing is based on the 1960 Kellys Directory, with dates expanded where a business stayed, or the trade stayed. Note where the date stops at 1976 this is only because that is the last year the directory was published. Residential properties are not included except where the house is of note or there were famous residents. The choice of 1960 means that our senior citizens will be able to reflect on their youth in Cosham, younger readers can see what was in the streets in 'olden' days, hopefully both groups will find something of interest within the booklet.

Streets which are listed as only residential are listed following with the dates first mentioned in planning minutes in brackets:
Aberdare Avenue (1927), **Bernard Avenue** (1932 Bailey & Whites)**, Chalkridge** Road (named in 1954)**, Chidham Road, The Close** (1935)**, Colville Road** (1933)**, Court Close** (named in 1955)**, Court Mead, Courtmount Grove** (1938/1946)**, Cranbourne Road** (named in 1954)**, Dean Road** (1929 extended in 1934)**, East Cosham Road, East Court, Glenleigh Avenue** (1935), **Knowsley Road, Lendorber Avenue** (Named by David Gammans, the builder & developer, after his children, Leonard, Doreen and Albert. Numbers 10-12 were rebuilt in 1947), **Lodge Avenue** (In 1932 Engelberg Avenue was renamed Lodge Avenue)**, Mansvid Avenue,** also named after Da*vid* Gam*mans*, **Merthyr Avenue** (1927), **The Orchard, Padwick Avenue** (1927)**, Pangbourne Avenue** (1937)**, Park Grove** (1933)**, Penrhyn Avenue** (1926), **Pervin Road** (extended in 1934)**, Regal Close** (In 1976 planning permission was granted for 3 blocks of flats for elderly and middle aged persons; Stuart, Tudor & Windsor Courts.)**, Rosebery Avenue** (was until 1934 known as No. 5 Road on the Salisbury Road Estate)**, Saint Colman's Avenue** (1927)**, Saint Matthews Road** (In 1897 the road is shown as Gladys Court)**, Southdown Road** (1933)**, Walberton Avenue** (new road by Stigant & Sons in 1929, 31 houses built in 1931)**, Widley Road, Widley Street, Widleyfield Road** (1933 houses to be built value not less then £750)**, Woolner Avenue**.

Albert Road
The road used to be numbered consecutively with 1,2,3,4...17 on the north side, now 1-33. 35 was Albert Villa, 37 Alberta House and 39 Mizpah House. The south side had Albert Terrace, 1-4, which became 12-18. Beyond that was a nursery now 30-38 and probably the car park at the end of the road. In 1928 4 houses were built by H.E Pitt.
North Side
Portsea Island Mutual Co-operative Society; Milk Depot; 1937 to 1976.
here is Pervin Road
35 W.W Burt; Builder; 1918 to 1960.
Later was W.W Burt & Co (Builders) Ltd; 1962 to 1967. Then A.J Fowler Ltd; Builders; 1971 to 1976.

here is Dean Road

Portsdown Masonic Hall Co Ltd; 1956 to 1976.

Earlier just listed as Masonic Hall; 1936 to 1953. The planning application was raised in 1935 by the Master of Portsdown Lodge.

“The Portsdown Lodge itself dates back to 1921. In 1926 they moved the meeting from the school to Cosham Institute, in Albert Road. The site of the Masonic Hall had been purchased in 1924. The hall was designed by Bro. Norman Scott and built by Messrs Clear & Sons. The opening meeting took place on 7th February 1936.”

www.portsdownlodge.org.uk where more details may be found.

The building has a carved stone “Masonic Hall 1935 ”. The building is now Portsdown Conference & Meeting Centre.

Albert Road, Masonic Hall

“In the 1940s mothers would take their children there for a free bottle of concentrated orange juice. It was a small bottle, about the same as a medicine bottle with a blue metal screw cap. The fact that the outside was always sticky it was probably filled on the premises. The place was always packed out with mothers and their children. ”

Malcolm Garlick

South Side
Portsmouth Dairies Ltd; 1948 to 1962.
Later Portsmouth Dairies became part of South Coast Dairies Ltd; 1964 to 1967, who in turn became part of Unigate Ltd (Home Counties Dairies Ltd); 1973 to 1976. A planning application was submitted for conversion to nursing home in 1986. Now Cosham Court Nursing Home.
The first commercial use seems to be as Foden's Ltd; Steam Wagon Depot; from 1928 to 1934. Later the building was used by United Services Garages (Portsmouth) Ltd; in 1938. Then in 1941 the premises were in use by Portsmouth, Southsea & Isle of Wight Aviation Ltd.
Primary School; 1946 to 1960.
Earlier shown as an Infants School; until to 1934. Court Lane Junior Mixed School, Annexe; 1962 to 1976. Later Further Education Centre. In 1997 planning application for ten houses submitted. Now Victoria Terrace.
Drill Hall: 1897 to 1971. (216th Hants Battery; 54th Wessex Brigade)
In 1986 a planning application was submitted for sheltered accommodation. Beatrice Mews now on the site.
28 Maurice Hawkins; Nurseryman; 1921 to 1960.
Earlier Thomas Hawkins; Nurseryman; 1911 to 1918.
In 1961 a planning application was submitted for 6 houses on the site.

Beaconsfield Avenue
Built in 1934 by Bailey & Whites Ltd, as street No3 on Salisbury Road Estate. Later renamed Beaconsfield Avenue.

Burrill Avenue
Formed from grounds of Cosham House, houses being built in 1927. The road was extended in 1933 by W.P Winter & Son Ltd.
East Side
22 E Ridge; Chartered Surveyor; 1958 to 1967.
here are Southdown Road and Colville Roads
West Side
Residential only

Cosham Park Avenue
Residential on north and south sides. The avenue leads to Cosham Park House Cosham Park at one time included grounds to the south to Knowsley Avenue,

and also included what later became Magdala Road and Dorking Crescent. The land was originally part of the Burrill estate and stretched south across the railway. The Burrill family sold the land in 1852 to Rev Henry Palmer who by 1861 was joined byWilliam Rawlinson and Henry Long. In 1870 the estate was sold to Rev Arthur Newman, James Denison and Clement Swanston. The estate included Cosham Park House, Dorney Court and Dorking House which were built over the years. Houses were built in the avenue in 1925 and 1926.

Cosham Park House, is Grade II listed, built in C19th, with 2 storeys, 3 bays verandah, 5 rooms on each floor. There were two cottages in the grounds for the coachman and gardener. The house had two driveways one at the south from the High Street near Knowsley Road, and another to the north just south of Magdala Road. The house does not seem to have been built for use by a local prominent family, but to generate an income as it was only leased for periods to various occupiers whose names are the ones that are in the trade directories. It was sold in 1923 to Mabel & Percy Tyler with Reginald Thomas Price, Cutler of Albert Road Southsea as sub-purchaser, but they still let the house. It was sold again in 1924 to Alfred Stretten who still leased the house. In 1929 Alfred Stretten put in a planning application to convert to flats. In 1937 he leased it for 8 years to Portsmouth Grammar School for use by boarders.

Mary Louise Streten of Catisfield House, Fareham; widow of Alfred Streten sold the house and land to Mayor, Aldermen and Citizens Of Portsmouth, (Portsmouth Corporation) for £3,350 on 21st August 1946 for use as the Junior Building School.

City of Portsmouth Building School; 1951 to 1958. Huts were built in the ground as extra classrooms in 1954. The building school relocated to London Road, Hilsea combining with other branches of the school.

Court Lane Secondary Modern School (Boys & Girls) Annexe; 1960.

City of Portsmouth; Portsdown & Hilsea Evening Institute; 1962 to 1975.

In 1974 it was transferred to Hampshire County Council under local government re-organisation.

North Portsmouth Further Education Centre; 1975 to 1976.

In 1993 under another local government re-organisation it was transferred to Highbury College.

Highbury College annexe; 1995.

Doctor's Surgery 1999 to 2017.

Court Lane
In 1923, 10 houses were built by G.H Nicholls, later in 1924 he also built bungalows in the lane. The road was widened in 1954.

East Side
For corner property see East Court in Havant Road
Court Lodge
Royston Hicks; Plumber/Builder;1946 to 1964.
Compton House

here are East Court, Court Mead, Court Close, Mansvid Avenue, Gofton Avenue, Langdale Avenue and Pangbourne Avenue.
New Cosham Sewage Works; 1938 to 1976.
In August 1933, the Lord Mayor opened new sewage disposal works at Cosham. These were built to cater for the 3,000 new homes that were to be built at Cosham.

West Side
here are Hilary Avenue, Beaconsfield Avenue, Lonsdale Avenue and Rosebery Avenue
W.H Hellier (Contractors) Ltd; Builders; 1960 to 1971.
John C Nicholls Ltd; Builders; 1951 to 1958, he lived in Compton House.
Auriol (Builders) Ltd; 1953 to 1958

Dorking Crescent
Earlier just one property listed, Dorking Cottage, this was demolished in 1958 and replaced with a bungalow. Since replaced with Broad Reach town houses?
North Side
In 1975 a planning application was raised for Vine Court, 9 flats at the rear of 20 Magdala Road.
In 1979 a planning application was raised for 6 one bedroom flats, Selwin Court at the rear of 22 Magdala Road.
In 1964 a planning application was raised for Megan Court, 24 one bed roomed flats in three blocks at rear of 24-30 Magdala Road. Built by Brown Bros of Roman House, Bitterne, architects Cogswell & Sons.

South Side
Dorking Garage (E.L Newman); Motor Engineers; 1953 to 1962.
Dorking Garage; Motor Engineers; 1964 to 1976.

Dysart Avenue

In 1952/4 the road was extended by Mr S Berney and 16 houses built in the avenue and Lower Drayton Lane.

North Side

In 1952, number 55, stables were converted into a house and garage. A newer bungalow number 57 has been built in front so little of the house is visible from the road.

"At the eastern end on the north corner now hidden behind modern housing were what was believed to be old farm buildings."

Malcolm Garlick

South Side

44 Dysart Avenue, Drayton Manor

A large 3 storey detached house partly faced in flint, with rendered western wall. Over the door of the porch in Dysart Avenue is a plaque with two crossed keys. High up on the wall of the main house and obscured by a creeper for most of the year is another plaque, the lettering on this seems to contain two capital S with another letter between them. See also the following notes.

Note the term manor does not apply to a house, as tends to be the use nowadays, but is an area of land. In some cases the owner did build a house within the area which became the manor house; if they already had a large house elsewhere and owned several manors then sometimes lodges were built for their local representative. In the following the text indicated *{text}* is inserted by WEA.

The manor/house is elusive in many ways:
Firstly in earlier references it is listed in (Lower) Drayton Lane, yet driving or walking down the lane there is only an old looking thing is a flint wall, which fronts the old lodge. So one might think that it was demolished in the 1950s as the houses seem to date from, which is partly true. To find what is left of the old manor house and outbuildings you have to turn into Dysart Avenue where just inside on the north and south what is left of the buildings can be seen.

Secondly there are three Drayton Manors in Hampshire; this one near Farlington; one near Barton Stacey which has connections to Hyde Abbey, Winchester; and another near Alresford with connections with St Peters Abbey, Winchester. So when finding references to Drayton Manor one has to be careful which of the three it is talking about.

Thirdly the history of the manor in this area varies depending on the reference book you read.

Taking the Victoria County History of 1908 as the major source of early history throughout the country:
The earliest mention of Drayton (Dreton) seems to be in the year 1250, when Henry III gave a moeity *{share}* of the land there to Roger de Merlay; and between 1250 and 1271 he seems to have given the remaining lands to Richard de Sandford. Roger gave his share in the lands which amounted to only four acres to Ralph atte Brigge from who they passed to Henry Wade. Richard died seised of twelve acres of land in Drayton in 1289 and the lands passed to his son and heir Thomas de Sandford . In 1303 Henry Wade granted his land to Thomas so that the whole estate was then owned by one family.
The land passed through many families: Pageham, Borrard (cousin of Pagehams), Pound (they also owned Farlington so the two manors were then held in common), Wayte; Earl of Sussex (by marriage to Honora Wayte), Garth, Wolfe, Hunt, Taylor. In 1815 the joint manors were sold by the trustees of Taylor's estates to Lord Keith who sold it in 1818 to John Walker Finally

in 1857 the joint manors were purchased from the Trustees of John Walker by John Deverell. At John Deverell's death in 1880 the manor passed to his son William. At the time of writing of the Victoria County History, in 1908, the manor of Farlington was still owned by the Deverell family and Drayton Manor House was the residence of Lieut-Col Alfred Thistlethwayte.

Hampshire Telegraph:
The owner of the manors seems to have been in trouble in 1829 as it is advertised in the Hampshire Telegraph for sale by auction, with the mansion at Purbrook, if failing to sale to be pulled down and materials sold.

Robert Bray in his Drayton Trail produced for local schools in 1987:
A stone, believed to be an original part of this first building showing the Crossed Keys of St Peter can be seen above the main porchway.
In the 16th Century, the land around the ruins was given as part of a bridal dowery and a Manor House was built using some of the original stones, High up on the front wall a stone plaque can be seen which shows the initials 'FEF' of the two families joined by this marriage. Most of the first Manor was destroyed by fire in the early 19th Century. A second manor was built in 1822 of which half remains. In about 1950 the right hand part *{western part}* was demolished. On a map of 1907 the manor, outbuildings and estate can be seen: the main house, the stables, the coach house and the lodge. *{The trail also claims the first building on this site was built in the C12th as Pilgrim's hostel for the Cistercian Order. However this conflicts with the Victoria County History and we have found no evidence to substantiate this claim.}*

White's Hampshire of Hampshire of 1878:
The Drayton descriptive entry states rebuilt in 1872 for Miss Secker, and it is described as a very handsome Elizabethan residence upon the site of the old Manor House. She is listed in the residents section at Drayton Manor. *{However, all other sources seem to agree on 1822 as the rebuilding.}*

Portsmouth City Council Minutes
The house was leased to Portsmouth Corporation for 10 years in 1945 for use as a mental home. In 1947, 1952 and then in 1953 there were various planning applications the last of which was for, numbers 36-42 Dysart Avenue, two pairs of houses after part demolition of the manor.
{This was carried out in 1957, hence the plain rendered wall on the west of the house. The coach house to the north of the estate was converted to a house, see number 55. The stables would have been where the modern

bungalow was built fronting Dysart Avenue.}
Memories:
"After the war when the army moved out in approx 1950. The grounds reached south to Old Manor Way at the bottom of Lower Drayton Lane where it met the farm in Grove Road."

"It was then in ruins before they started making it into flats. When I was 14, I used to clamber up the stairs and under the eaves to the roof with Bob & Verna. There used to be a secret passage under the window seat, but it is filled in now."

Havant Road
Earlier the section from London Road to Park Lane was East Street. Between Park Lane and Mulberry Lane there was then no road as the main road went south down Park Lane then returned north via Mulberry Lane. This gave the name Crooked Cosham to this part of Cosham.
North Side
1 Red Lion Taxis; 1958 to 1967.
Miles Taxis (D.J Miles); 1948 to 1956.
3A Harry Rook; Motor Engineer; 1953 to 1960.
"He sold motorcycles and spares for the same. It was a very strange building inside, I think it was split level with very heavy roof supports."
Malcolm Garlick

29 G.P Kelsey & Son; Boot Repairs; 1937 to 1962.
Earlier George Kelsey; Boot Repairs; 1936.
39 Charles Rayner; Confectioner; 1951 to 1964.
Had been a confectioner for many years with Mrs R Owen; Confectioner; 1938 to 1940 and John Owen; Confectioner; 1946 to 1948.
41 H.G Luker; Pastrycook; 1958 to 1962.
Had been a Café for may years with: Misses Kemp & Lyne; Café; 1938 to 1940: Misses Blackbourn & Lyne; Café; 1946: Cinderella's Café; Mrs B.I Blackbourn & Mrs G.M Morgan; 1948: Cinderella Café; H.G Luker; 1951 to 1956.
here is Widley Street
1-41 Havant Road and Widley Street have all been demolished.
Just after Widley Street used to be another public house, The Pure Drop, listed in the 1881 census as the Pure Drop Beerhouse, Ellen Windebank.

here is St Matthews Road

55 Derek Robertson Duff; Physician & Surgeon; 1951 to 1964.
Earlier the same house is listed as 53 with J Hamilton Bell; Physician & Surgeon; 1928 to 1936: Bell, Doyle & Sladen; 1937. Renumbered to 55 with Bell, Doyle & Sladen; Physicians & Surgeons; 1938 to 1940: J Hamilton Bell; Physician & Surgeon; 1946 to 1948.
The house has since been demolished and 4 houses, 55a-d Havant Road built on the site, planning application 1965.
Walberton Court, sheltered housing built in 1987.

here is St Colman's Avenue

St Colman's Roman Catholic Church; 1936 to 2017. (See cover for photo.)
Listed as St Colman's Roman Catholic Church; 1934.
Blessed and opened on 25th November 1928 by Bishop Cotter. St Colman was the patron saint of his native diocese of Cloyne in County Cork, Ireland. Note the chequer board patterning of the stonework.
A planning application was raised in 1935 for the church hall.
Earlier a property known simply as The Cottage, stood here; 1892 to 1905 Mrs O'Shea; 1911 to 1925 Misses O'Shea. The church was built in the garden of the cottage. One of the sisters later lived at 53; 1923.

"On the Northern side of Havant Road and immediately facing Park Lane stood, until very recently, a house known as The Cottage which was at the beginning of the 20th century the home of the O'Shea sisters. They were well known in the village as doers of good works. The elder sister, Nora, however, achieved some national fame as an ardent worker for women's rights. She organised open-air meetings and raised funds for the cause. The sisters are still remembered by the people living in Cosham. There is general agreement that they died penniless having given their money away. The house was subsequently lived in by Dr Bell who is also fondly remembered. The land on which the Roman Catholic Church was erected in 1929 was formerly the garden of the house. Prior to this date the cottage, which probably dated from the early 19th century was the home of the Curtis family. Admiral Sir Roger Curtis was the owner of the Gatcombe Park Estate at Hilsea, he was required to sell his estate to the army in 1813. His youngest son Rear Admiral Sir Lucius Curtis Bart, moved to East Cosham. He married Mary Figg Greetham the daughter of Mr Moses Greetham."

Sylvia Webb

here is Widley Road (Earlier Widleyfield Lane, 1895) Now Widley Road

Footpath.
Cosham House Lodge, later 59.

William Young; 1925 to 1948.

Padwick House, later 63.

Was used by Edward Sladen, Physician & Surgeon, from 1934 to 1971 as his surgery. Still named Padwick House.

here is Padwick Avenue

69 Cosham House; a large house with 2 Storeys & 5 bays with verandah, Grade II listed which may have been built in the 1840s replacing an earlier house. William Padwick, senior, is listed here from 1812 to 1834 when he died aged 66. Other local politicians and business people later lived there. One of the last residents was Robert Winnicott the head of the local building company from 1924 to 1971. In 2017 the house still stands in its own grounds, although it was converted into flats in 1924 by Robert Winnicott.

Robert Winnicott founded his building business at Copnor Road in 1904 where the firm remained until they moved to Rowlands Castle in 1975. He was the Lord Mayor of Portsmouth in 1946. It is rumoured that Winston Churchill stayed at the house around the time of the D-Day landings. Robert died in 1971. His great-grandsons still run the business at Rowlands Castle.

here are Burrill Avenue and Bernard Avenue

On 1867 map Cosham Lodge is shown between Cosham House and East Cosham House. One of the prominent occupiers was in the 1860s Admiral Lucius Curtis.

The house was demolished in 1920s: Anida Rayfield states in her book Discovering Cosham.

Verden Victor L Dashwood; Dashwood & Sons; Funeral Directors; 1937. Later numbered 81; Victor L Dashwood; Dashwood & Sons; Funeral Directors; 1938 to 1964. The house is still there as a private house with no name, just 81.

here is Lodge Avenue

89/91 East Cosham House:

A C18th 2 storey, 4 bay house with verandah, Grade II listed.

One of the early residents was Sir George Garrett of East Cosham House, died 15th April 1832, aged 60. He was a brewer in Old Portsmouth. Another resident was in 1839 Admiral Patterson who was succeeded by his son-in law, Sir William Wiseman, Baronet. He married, Charlotte Jane, the only daughter of Admiral Patterson on the 25th October 1838 at Widley Church. This was in the old village that was to the north of Fort Widley that has been abandoned. William Hellier a local builder lived there from 1953 to 1966. The house was for sale in 1981. It is now a residential home for the elderly, East Cosham House.

here is East Cosham Road
The Goodwyns:
On the 1867 Ordnance Survey map the building is shown with no name.
In the 1881 census, Goodwyn House; James Woodward; Provision Merchant and Farmer of 25 acres, employing 2 men and 1 boy is listed.
The house was rebuilt in 1932 for Samuel Isted, in mock tudor style. However, Anida Rayfield in her book Discovering Cosham states that some parts were earlier.
The house had extensive grounds. It was last used as Mulberry Park Children's Nursery (Goodwyns Ltd), 1998 to 2012.
It was demolished, along with outbuildings in the grounds.
A Churchill Retirement homes development, Simmonds Lodge, has been erected on the site.

95 East Goodwyns;1934 to 1937.
"It was owned by G.A Day and always has plenty of blue election posters up at election times."
Malcolm Garlick
The house is still there.

Beyond this was East Cosham Farm.
In 1924 the land on the north side of Havant Road and west of Drayton Lane was still owned by Winchester College and was for sale by auction.

South Side
6-38 have been demolished.
6 N.A & M Read; Newsagents, Stationers & Tobacconists; 1958 to 1967.
Earlier Frederick Milmer; Newsagent & Tobacconist; 1934 to 1940: Frank Summerfield; Newsagent; 1946 to 1948: Miss G.M Frankham; Confectioner; 1951:
Dodd & Read; Newsagents; 1951 to 1956.
"I delivered newspapers for Milmers, my round took me around east Cosham on Sundays. I returned to the shop to find I was delivering papers to the Q.A Hospital which was full of wounded service men in

those days. I had names I had never heard of before and if I went past a bed I would think the patient was sleeping"
Arthur Collins

8 Mrs R.E Stoves; Confectioner; 1960.
Earlier Robert Pearce; Confectioner; 1936 to 1940: Miss F Grant; Confectioner; 1946 to 1948: Mrs G.M Hewett; Confectioner; 1953 to 1958.
Later Reuben Caplan; Confectioner; 1962 to 1964.
Mrs I.V.V Rennison; Confectioner; 1966 to 1967.

12 W.E Brown; Hairdresser; 1953 to 1967.

28 Was earlier used by a basket making family, the Fullicks for four generations.
Fullick; 1850; Basket Shop, Havant Road.
John Fullick; 1875; Sieve Maker & Seedsman
Mrs Charlotte Fullick; 1878, Sieve Maker & Seed Dealer
Mrs Fullick; 1885; Sieve Maker & Seedswomen
James Cooper, 1886; Basket & Sieve Maker - James was the second husband of Charlotte Fullick, nee Cooper.
J.R.R Cooper; 1888; Basket Maker.
Edward Fullick; 1896 to 1932; Basket & Sieve Maker.
The building was sold by Mrs H Peacock in 1964 to a development company.

here is Widley Square, now Old Market Road.

38 Uncle Tom's Cabin:
There has been a beerhouse / public house here for many years sometimes named, sometimes not. The Porter family were here from 1875 to 1905, starting with William, then passing to his wife, Elizabeth and finally their daughter Louisa. Charles Mills and later his wife were here from 1923 to 1940. After that there is a succession of landlords until 1967.
In 1934 it was a Gales house, they made alterations in 1955.

"Father and Mother and brother and I would always take a Sunday afternoon early evening walk, and end up in a pub. The Cabin was popular because there was a swing in the garden and my brother and I would go there with a bottle of lemonade with straw and packet of Smith's crisps."
Sylvia Webb

"The beer was served from barrels at the rear of the bar"
Patricia Cleal

Cosham Baptist Church; 1921 to 2017.
The first Baptist Church was built in 1871. On the 1873 Ordnance Survey map it is shown as East Cosham Chapel (Baptist). The church has since had modern extensions built at the front and has been changed again, see below.

48 East Cosham Tavern; 1871 to 1976.
Dates back to at least 1864 when it was owned by Cox's Brewery of Landport. None of the landlords seem to have stayed for any length of time.
It was rebuilt in 1968 and renamed Uncle Tom's Cabin.
Uncle Tom's Cabin; 1971 to 1976. The pub was converted into meeting rooms for the Baptist Church in 2002.

here is Havant Place

56 Preedy, Gardiner & Co Ltd; Motor Garage; 1960 to 1964.
Earlier T.J Chinneck; Motor Engineer; 1923 to 1928: Young Harry's Motor Coaches; 1934: Henry E Collins; Motor Engineer; 1936 to 1938:
Portsdown Motor Co (Portsmouth) Ltd; 1940 to 1946: N Letton & Co Ltd; Motor Garage; 1948 to 1958.
Now Admirals Place, flats, 54-60 Havant Road, planning application raised in 2001.

60A Mrs E.A Bath; Coal & Coke Merchant; 1958 to 1971.
Earlier listed at 58; Mrs Elizabeth Bath; Greengrocer; 1936 to 1940:
Mrs Elizabeth Bath; Coal Merchant; 1946 to 1956.
Later Bath & Sons; Coal Merchants; 1973 to 1976.

62 Has been a wine merchants for many years.
Wallace Pugsley; Wine, Spirit & Beer Merchant; 1934 to 1940.
V.S Pugsley; Wine Merchant; 1946 to 1948.
Pugsley's Ltd; Wine Merchants; 1951 to 1953.
Smeeds Ltd; Wine Merchants; 1956 to 1967.
62a Now Cosham Glass & Timber; 62b Executive Property Maintenance; 62c Oriental Food Market.

here is Park Lane

66 Albert Vaughan; General Store; 1951 to 1960.
Earlier Albert Vaughan; Confectioner; 1936 to 1948.
Later H Fitzjohn; General Store; 1962 to 1964: N.D Offer; Grocer; 1966 to 1967: Lewis's; Newsagents; 1973 to 1975. Now Oxygen

Newsagents.

68A Alfred Hatter; Boot Repairs; 1948 to 1962.
Later Stoneham Bros; Shoe Repairs; 1964 to 1976. Now Portsmouth Models.

78 Southlands; Albert Coffin; 1934 to 1937.
78; Albert Coffin; 1938 to 1964.
78 Then has a variety of owners
1979 Planning application for 14 houses.

84 Leslie Walker-Powell; Surgeon Dentist; 1946 to 1964.

86 Southsea Snapshots Ltd; Commercial Photographers; 1951 to 1973.

here are Mulberry Lane, Woolner Avenue and Lendorber Avenue

118-124

Now Atkinson Court, a development of 40 extra care retirement flats. The WEA Local History Group were asked to suggest a name and Atkinson Court was suggested.

Thomas Atkinson joined the navy as an Able Seaman in 1787 on board HMS Colossus, within a few years he had become a Masters Mate and he obtained his Masters Certificate in 1795. He served on several ships including HMS Theseus, which at that time was the Flagship of Lord Nelson and he was with Nelson for a period of eight years before Trafalgar.

He was the Master and senior warrant officer on board HMS Victory during the Battle of Trafalgar (1805). He was at this time 37 years old. It was his task with his crew to actually sail and steer the ship. He held his rank by warrant rather than commission. He joined HMS Victory on the 14th April 1803. During the Battle, the Victory had her wheel shot away and with 40 sailors he steered the ship from the lower decks using a tiller and system of blocks and tackles.

Upon leaving HMS Victory after the Battle of Trafalgar he took up the post of Master Attendant of Halifax Dockyard, Nova Scotia.

After leaving Halifax Dockyard he became First Master Attendant of Portsmouth Dockyard where he died in 1836 aged 68. He is buried in St Andrews churchyard Farlington where there is a memorial stone.

His inscription reads (in part):

> 'To the memory of Thomas Atkinson Esq late first Master Attendant HM Dockyard Portsmouth, who departed this life the 2nd day of June 1836. He was Master of several of Admiral Nelsons Flagships including 'Victory' at the battle of Trafalgar'.

Earlier 120 was converted into a rest home, planning application 1986. In 1989 number 122 was added, later 124 was added. In 2004 application was submitted to demolish 120-124 former nursing home. In 2004 a new application was submitted for a block of 46 sheltered apartments by McCarthy and Stone.

here is Court Lane

East Court Lodge:

Just called the Lodge on the 1867 Ordnance Survey map with East Court Farm to the south in Court Lane.

In 1969 it was sold and demolished along with adjoining Compton House which was the 16th cent farmhouse. Development was to be by Hayes & Middlesex Construction Co Ltd.

"A very imposing building set in large grounds. I visited it only once to a much publicised local fete which was held in the 1940s. Lots of people, flags and stalls come to mind. Whether it was something to do with the the war ending I do not know. I know I had not started school, so that would date it to about 1946."

Malcolm Garlick

Hilary Avenue

1934 New road No.2 on Salisbury Road Estate to be named Hilary Avenue. Numbers 23-29 were rebuilt in 1945 after war damage.

North Side

Court Lane Secondary Modern School for Boys & Girls; 1956 to 1960.
Later Court Lane Junior Mixed School; 1962 to 1975.
Later Court Lane First & Middle School; 1976.
Later Manor Court Secondary School Annexe; 1962 to 1976

"The school itself has not changed much except for the eastern end where the infants area now stands. The largish concrete buildings stood on the northern boundary, one was a sort of science laboratory and the other eventually became the girls cookery classroom. At the far of the eastern end was a lot of waste ground known to us as the 'bumps'. We were not allowed to play on them but boys being boys we were often in trouble.

The school was segregated at the time with the dividing line being the grassy area in the middle of the playground with the boys having the playground east of the grass while the girls had that to the west plus the grass itself. We were not allowed to mix. A popular game at the time was known as Dare, Truth, Love, Kiss or Promise. It seemed to be played only by the boys and when it was your turn you had to pick from one of the five options. Nine times out of ten you would opt for dare. This was inevitably translated into we dare you to run onto the grass and kiss so and so! Good fun and I can't remember anybody ever getting into trouble for it. The headmaster was Mr Dunstan. My class teacher was Mr Butler (all the mums liked him). Other teachers were Mr Woodhill, Mr Stephens (Music) and Mr Ramsey (Local Studies & Science)."

Malcolm Garlick

Council School; 1937 to 1940

Later Primary School; 1946 to 1976.

Later Manor Court Secondary Modern (Boys & Girls); 1971 to 1976.

Court Lane Infant School; 2014; largely rebuilt over the last ten years, but with four classrooms dating back to 1930.
Court Lane Junior School; 2017

"Apart from the Goodwyns the other venue for the teenagers was Manor Court Youth Club in Drayton, which is where I learnt to play guitar. It was lively and there were plenty of activities to choose from. After the youth club we would retire to the New Inn for refreshments. In those days it was a really popular pub with lounge bar and saloon. It had a fairly large lounge and we could be all be found there, drinking a jar or two."

Frank Thompson

South Side
Residential only.

Knowsley Crescent

On the 1873 Ordnance Survey Map this is shown as South Road. In 1930 the road off Knowsley Road was to be named Knowsley Crescent.

Knowsley Road

14 houses and a bungalow were planned by builder B Rea, 2 houses by W.J Carter in 1924. The road was extended in 1925 and again in 1926.
North Side
Residential only

South Side

Bilboe & Clibbery Ltd; Printers & Commercial Stationers; 1940 to 1976.

"On the railway side just before the Railway Inn was a stationers called Bilboe & Clibberry, I seem to recall it was painted cream all over. They were always good for writing books, such as a new notebook for jotting down railway engine numbers etc. Between them and the houses was the fence alongside the railway goods yard."

Malcolm Garlick

Erith & Co Ltd; Builders' Merchants; 1956 to 1976.
Now Jewson; Builders' Merchants, 2017

Langdale Avenue

North Side
13 Mrs S.C Perry; Private School; 1953 to 1976.
South Side
Residential only

Lendorber Road

Houses by A.J Chase and G Brown in 1925, with more following in 1926.

Lindisfarne Close

Beamond Court was built to the south of land that was part of Southlands, Havant Road. In 2011 the building was refurbished as Eliza MacKenzie Court by The Agamemnon Housing Association.

Lonsdale Avenue

Part of the Salisbury Estate which was built in 1937. Lonsdale Avenue was built by Percy Frere.
North Side
Residential only.
South Side
The Salisbury public house, built in 1937 for Portsmouth & Brighton United Breweries. Until recently a Wadsworth house, now converted into a Co-op convenience shop.

2 Chusan Stores; 1960 to 1976; Grocer
Earlier Mrs Mary Dovey; 1958; Grocer: Herbert Kinch; 1937 to 1956; Grocer.

Lonsdale Road, The Salisbury

here is Roseberry Avenue

Magdala Road

"My Uncle Bill Lewis lived in Magdala Road before the war. He was a wholesale newsagent and had to go Fratton Station at 4 o'clock every morning to collect the papers. Somebody took exception to being woken up as he went by motorbike because he came back one morning and a wire had been stretch across the road. Luckily he was only caught across the chest rather than his neck because although he was injured he survived."

Janet Halls

North Side

27 C.J Gutteridge & Son Ltd; Builders; 1953 to 1976.
Now part of Orford Court, flats on site of 25-27.

Glenleigh Court, flats dating from 1968 are on the corner with Glenleigh Avenue.

here is Glenleigh Avenue

49 R.D Reddy; Physician & Surgeon; 1956 to 1960.
51 Dorney Court, earlier a large villa:

Shown on Ordnance Survey map in 1873.
It was mainly occupied by military families before passing through a variety of owners
Dorney Court, Flats; 1965 to 2017.
Park Mansions; 1948 to 1976:
In 1946 planning permission was granted for a block of 21 flats at Magdala Road / Park Lane for S.J Kelly. More recently in 2011 planning permission was granted for an extra storey.
here is Park Lane

South Side
14-16 Now Myfanwy, an Abbeyfield Society house.
A planning application was raised in 1968 for number 16 to be used as an Abbeyfield House.
Number 14 was earlier Park Lodge, 1885 to 1918. In 1982 a planning application was raised to change of use to be combined with number 16 as an Abbeyfield House. The property had 11 flats for the over 60s. It is now being demolished to be replaced by a new purpose built block.
here is Dorking Crescent
42 Victor Martindale; Physician & Surgeon; 1951 to 1971.
Earlier:
Dorking House was shown on the Ordnance Survey map in 1873. It was lived in by various military families and local businessmen.
Demolished and replaced with three terraced houses 42a-c 1973.
here are Dorking Crescent and Widley Court Drive.
Hartington Lodge is shown on the Ordnance Survey maps in 1873.
Hartington House; in 1878; Rev Charles Coar
It was later known as Parkstone House, with various military and naval residents. Later still it became Widley Court and was the home of George Hall King for 40 years.
In 1952 a planning application was raised for conversion to 4 flats by R.J Winnicott Ltd.
Widley Court; 2017; now three flats in the old house.

here are Salisbury Road and Mulberry Lane

Widley Court

Mulberry Lane

The 'newer' houses started to be built in 1927, the road was named in 1930.

East Side

here is Mulberry Avenue

15 Mulberry House:

Shown on early map, 1867 as Knapps. Later, by 1875 it was known as The Mulberries.

The wall forming the boundary of Mulberry House, Church and pavement was built in 1954 by the council to enable pavement to be laid.

Cosham Congregational Church; 1934 to 1971.

Cosham United Reformed Church; 1973 to 1976.

In 1933 a planning application was made for a church hall.

In 1959 another planning application was made for new church at The Close, Mulberry Lane. The church was on the corner of Mulberry Lane and The Close, with the hall at the rear on the north side of the Close.

In February 1961 the new Congregational Church was opened in Mulberry Lane, cost £15,500. Monies coming from Christchurch, Southsea and Edinburgh Road Churches plus local fund raising.
In 1963 there was a planning application for the demolition of the church hall and erection of a new single storey hall. In 2007 there was an application for 7 houses to be built after demolition of the church and halls.
The Church combined with the Methodist Church at Drayton.

Mulberry House

19 House rebuilt after bomb damage 1945.
21 House rebuilt after bomb damage 1946.
here is The Close - built in 1935.
here are Salisbury and Magdala Roads

West Side
Residential only.

Park Lane
On the Ordnance Survey Maps of 1873 to 1910 this is shown as Upper Park

Lane with Victoria Villas on the west side.
East Side
2 C Lewis; Grocer; 1960 to 1975. The shop is first listed as a dairy in 1934. Later Bath & Sons; Coal Merchants & Grocers; 1976.
30 Rebuilt 1946.
here are Magdala & Salisbury Roads

West Side
49 Albert Stewart Ashley; Furniture Removers; 1934 to 1960.
Later Ashley's; Furniture Removers; 1964 to 1976. EarlierAlbert is listed in 1931 and 1932 at number 8.

St George's Road
The houses started to be built in 1927.

"Number 8 was home to Cliff Parker the Pompey footballer who played in the 1939 FA cup."

Malcolm Garlick

North Side, residential only
South Side
10 Miss V.M Terry; Chiropodist & Masseuse; 1960 to 1964.

St John's Road
West Side
11 John Norman Sampson; Physician & Surgeon; 1953 to 1976.
East, North and South sides, residential only

Salisbury Road
On the Ordnance Survey maps from 1867 to 1879 this is shown as Water Lane. By 1897 Salisbury Road. There were two houses on the west side, St Bertha's and St Anns. The houses on the odd side seem to have been developed in the 1910s. The planning application for No.17 was raised by John Day, builder, in 1955.

East Side
here is Mulberry Lane
Church of the Nazarene; 1951 to 2017, Wesleyan Evangelical.
Listed as a Mission Room; 1936 to 1948.
The planning application 1935 was allowed despite being not within zone, i.e not housing.

Church of the Nazarene

Although Wesleyan the church is not connected with the Methodist church but is part of the International Church of the Nazarene an evangelical movement in the Wesleyan tradition that was founded in 1908 on the Pacific coast of the USA.

here are Hilary Avenue and Beaconsfield Avenue

14 later 27

"Having paid off our mortgage in 2011 we received copies of all the documents pertaining to the property. The first mention is in 1875 when two pieces of land at Cosham Park, plots 83 & 84 were conveyed from C.J Swanston, Esq to Mr Frederick Strickland. Only two days later Frederick passed the land on to C Richardson. Charles Richardson died on 19th December 1885 leaving the land to his nephew Adolphus Richardson. The plots passed through a few more owners until in 1913 a 50 feet wide plot was sold to Christopher Claud Coles of Oakley, Salisbury Road by Miss Rose Cowper of Laurel Cottage, Cosham for £133. This mentions the piece of land forming part of lot 83 in Cosham Park on the west side of a road formerly called Eastern Road and now called Salisbury Road, 38 feet frontage and depth 101 feet. (So another name, Water Lane, Eastern Road, Salisbury Road). One difficulty is researching the history has been the numbering of houses, on the west side there were even numbers from north to south. Number 2 became number 43 and number 14 became 27. The road was renumbered in 1935 by Portsmouth City Council as new houses had been built on the east side north from Lonsdale Avenue."

Martin de Klerk

16 William George Evans; Decorator & Builder; 1948 to 1967.
here is Lonsdale Avenue

Mission Room; 1937 to 1976.

Youth Centre; 1951. This was held in an old Nissen hut erected here.

Goodwyns Youth Centre; 1953 to 1967.

Moat Club, 1971 to 1976.

"I remember Goodwyns Youth Club, which was located in the road behind the Salisbury public house, and was run by Norman Barker. Remembered by many teenagers as a kind and easy going character. In particular I remember the juke box in the coffee bar and how it would thump out the sounds of the early sixties. The club also has a games room with snooker and table tennis, plus a large hall which was used for dances at the weekends. The dances always featured local groups with their 'vox' box amplifier and electric guitars. On dance nights the car park was filled with Triumphs, BSAs, Royal Enfields all good old British Motorcycles."

Frank Thompson

The mission room was built by F Faulkner in 1936 for the Plymouth Bretheren. It was sold in 2013 and is now Gary Sadler Physiotherapy.

A new Bretheren Meeting Hall has been built to the south.

Cosham Allotments Association, these are on the site of the former Cosham Water Works.

West Side
Residential only.
Earlier Cosham Gas Works were here 1895.

There was a cottage known as Gas Works Cottage. In a recent publication a 1930s photo shows it with the walls slate hung and captioned since demolished. However, Gas Cottage was altered in 1975 according to planning applications and a porch added sometime before 1987. It still stands and is known as Lamplighters Cottage. The name is over the doorway on the entrance porch and on gable end is a painted date 1874. The walls are now rendered.

Lamp Lighters Cottage, Salisbury Road

Tregaron Avenue

In 1948 6 houses were planned by Cosham Estates Ltd. Later in 1952 6 shops were proposed on the corner of Old Manor Way and Tregaron Avenue; and 20 houses in Old Manor Way by F.G Trewen Ltd. This was superceded in 1956 by a plan for 7 shops and 6 flats by the East Court Trust.

"My Auntie Nin lived in a big posh house in Tregaron Avenue off of Havant Road. She had a grand driveway and staircase. I remember seeing my grandma there; playing dress up; my aunt had

a pekinese called Mintin which she buried under an oak tree at the bottom of the garden. She had a large larder and she would always give me a bag of colonial sugar.
She kept a lot of china and silver behind glass in cabinets, and had a grand piano. She was a friend of my mum and baby sat us when mum and dad went out."
Susannah Kimber

East Side
Residential Only
West Side
Residential except for the southern end
here is Mansvid Avenue
48 PIMCO; 1960 to 1976. The planning application for the shop was raised in 1955. Still a coop shop in 2017.
48a Fiona Fayre, Ladies' Hairdresser; 1964 to 1976. Now Tregaron Hair Design.
50 W Durant & Son, Butchers; 1962 to 1967. W.S Wood, Butcher, 1971 to 1976. Now A.M Shepperd Ltd; Butcher, Established 1989
52 Colwin (Hardware) Ltd, Hardware Dealers; 1962 to 1964. P & D Walker, Hardware; 1966 to 1967. T.B & J Brinton, Hardware Stores; 1971 to 1976. Now MSL Computers Ltd. A family run business for over 15 years.
54 Manor Fruits, Greengrocers; 1962 to 1976. Now Cosham Balti; Takeaway; owner Mahmud Hussain for over 21 (2013) years.
56 Jarman, Tobacconist; 1962 to 1964. R Keys, Newsagent; 1967 to1976. Now Blades of Drayton, Hairdresser.

Widley Court Drive
On the 1873 Ordnance Survey Map this is shown as Windsor Road and carried on to Knowsley Road.
Named Widley Court Drive in 1952. In 1953 2 houses built by R.J Winnicott.

"Our journey from Highbury to Court Lane School was via Windsor Road railway bridge. Things were a lot less safety conscious in those days and one of the stupid pranks was to climb down onto the railway tracks and place an old halfpenny on the rails just before a train came along. If we were lucky, the coin stayed in place and the engine went over it. When the train had passed we would go out and find the coin

which was now larger in diameter and a lot thinner. In our more sensible moments we restricted our spare time to collecting train numbers. It was all steam in those days.
Coming home was usually the reverse route but occasionally we would take the long way via Widley Court Drive. In the 1950s this was nothing more than a track along the back of the houses in Salisbury Road. The west side of the path was waste ground with a tennis court which I never saw used. The track joined Knowsley Road by means of an alley between the houses."

Malcolm Garlick

Wootton Street
Not listed in 1960.

The second part of our booklet covers part of the area off Portsea Island known as Drayton, covering from Drayton Lane to Farlington Avenue, the railway line to hill slopes.

The Victoria County History of 1908 mentions the hamlet of Drayton is gradually developing into a residential locality. To the north past the New Inn is the Drayton building estate on which new villas are rising steadily. To the south is Drayton Manor, the residence of Lieut-Col Alfred Robert William Thistlethwayte.

The Drayton Manor Estate was developed by D Gammans in 1936 with 429 houses, 6 shops and 7 new roads the following year. Further roads, Braemar Avenue and Invergordon Avenue, were laid out or extended in 1946 by Portsmouth Modern Housing Ltd.

The streets following were listed as residential only in 1960. The dates in brackets are when the street is first mentioned in planning applications. **Aberdare Avenue, Beaconsfield Avenue, Braemar Avenue** (1937)**, Brecon Avenue** (1928)**, Carmarthen Avenue, Carshalton Avenue** (1930)**, Central Road** (Until 1950 was Central Road and Central Road West)**, Chilgrove Road** (1935), **Drayton Close** (new road off Lower Drayton Avenue in 1955), **Dysart Avenue** (1937)**, Gofton Avenue** (1937)**, Hilltop Crescent** (1937), **Homefield Road** (named after the farm field), **Invergordon Avenue** (1937)**, Kinross Crescent** (1937, ditch at rear filled-in in 1953)**, Kirton Road** (1936), **Lampeter Avenue** (was to be Talgarth or Lampeter Avenue, David Gammans)**, Mansvid Avenue,** (1937, named after Da***vid*** Gam***mans***), **Merthyr Avenue, Montrose Avenue** (1937), **Old Manor Way** (1937, 1952 extended between Invergordon Road and Lower Drayton Lane)**, Old Rectory Road, Penarth Avenue**, **Scholars Close** (named after the school at the south)**, Southbourne Avenue** (new road off Lower Drayton Lane in 1955)**,Waverley Road** (2 pairs of houses 1933 by W.J Keeping).

Drayton Lane
This narrow lane is a guide to what the old roads in the area would have looked like before being developed and widened with pavements to meet modern building regulations. At the top of the lane on the east is what remains of Collyers Pit earlier used as chalk and flint pit. Cliff Cottages dating back to the 1820s used to stand in the old pit.

Grove Road

Flint House, in 1937 was bought for use as a Remand Home, near Grove Road. The lake and orchard grounds to be separated off. It may have been Drayton Cottage. The pond in the grounds was filled in with spoil from Cosham drainage works in 1951. The house was closed in 1953. The footpath alongside to Grove Road was opened in 1954. There is an area of waste ground between Grove Road and Karen Avenue which maybe where the house was.

> "Flint House was a childrens' home situated in its own grounds on the south side of Grove Road and between Lower Drayton Lane and Station Road. Two of the boys were in my class at Solent Road School. They always wore grey trousers and jerkins. I got on quite well with them. One became a good friend but I lost track of him not long after. In the mid 1950s the now derelict house became a hangout for teenagers. I believe the house was pulled down in the 1960s"
>
> Malcolm Garlick

Havant Road

North Side

97 A planning application was raised in 1959 for change of use from dwelling house to Roman Catholic Nunnery.
Convent of the Ladies of Mary; 1960 to 1975.
Sacred Heart Convent; 1976.
Since closed and sold for housing.

105 David Rossiter; Physician & Surgeon; 1951 to 1960.

here is Carmarthen Avenue

> "Near the junction with Carmathen Avenue was the old Portsmouth Boundary Stone. I think this disappeared in the 1980s."
>
> Malcolm Garlick

107 Carrick Court, retirement housing by McCarthy & Stone, planning application 2007.

The next two houses are set back from the road with a newer development to the east, Orchard Gate, 4 flats and 5 houses, planning application 2006.

109A Ernest Hibberd; Builder; 1948 to 1967.

109A C.F Hole; Fruit Merchant; 1953 to 1960.
Earlier Worthing Fruit & Flower Co Ltd; Potato Merchants; 1948 to 1951.

111-113 Southern Garages (Cosham) Ltd; Motor Engineers; 1940 to 1966.
Later Linningtons (Cosham) Ltd; Motor Agents; 1967 to 1971.
Now Meridien Milano, car sales.

here is Penarth Avenue

123a In 1982 a planning application was raised for a bungalow and garage in the rear garden of 123. The Hideaway.

Keats Lodge Built for Lieut George Lyne by Cortis & Hankins in 1925. Later became 123, still known as Keats Lodge.

Whitlands Alistair Mead; Physician & Surgeon; 1932 to 1937
Later numbered 129 then 127; Alistair Mead; Physician & Surgeon; 1938 to 1962. Still there but called Thistledown House.

here is Penrhyn Avenue

The Broadway; 1928 only 1-4, by 1934 1 to 14. Pairs of shops built in 1926 by JEJ as on the plaque on 151-153.

129-131 Earlier 13-14 The Broadway.
Bernard Leslie Light; Hardware Stores; 1934 to 1960.
B.L Light & Son; Ironmongers; 1962 to 1976.
129 Now Northwood Estate Agents
131 Now Natural Choice Wood Floors.

135 Earlier 12 The Broadway
Portsea Island Mutual Co-operative Society Ltd; Grocers; 1934 to 1976.
Now Wood Floors.

137 Earlier 11 The Broadway
Portsea Island Mutual Co-operative Society Ltd; Butchers; 1936 to 1976.
135-137 Havant Road, the Co-op having relocated to the other side of the road the premises are now Kassia, Indian Tapas Bar, part of the Red Lounge Group. Another branch is in Osborne Road, Southsea.

139-141 Was earlier a Civic Restaurant in 1951 a planning application was raised to convert the building into 3 lock-up shops.
139 Pet Supplies; 1953 to 1966. Now Fry & Kent; Estate Agents.
141 James Wynn; Cycle Agent; 1953 to 1962. Earlier at 151; 1938 to 1951. Now Fine & Country; Estate Agents.

"In the 1940s Drayton was one of my family's first stops for everyday shopping etc. It had a shop for just about everything you would need for day to day living. My main memory of the village was a toy shop named Wynns. When I first started using it, it was situated near a a first class chippy (still in use - see 161). The shop then moved a few doors along to larger premises at 141 Havant Road. I was a bit spoilt as a child and Mr Wynn got to know my parents and myself quite well. We were always in there buying Dinky Toys, Hornby Dublo railway stuff and Meccano. Around 1952 he asked me to build a large Meccano tower to display in his window as an advert but unfortunately we left the area for good before I could get around to doing it. He also sold push bikes, new and second hand. Some of the latter were leaned against a telegraph pole, not locked, on the edge of the pavement. My Dad bought my second hand two wheeled bike from him, a Hercules Jeep, for £3. It lasted for several years."

Malcolm Garlick

141A H.G Ruston; House Furnishers, Upholsterer, Bedding etc; 1953 to 1966.

143 Earlier 10 The Broadway
George A Cooper, Dairy; 1937 to 1938.
G.B Cooper; Butcher; 1948 to 1960.
Now Southern Counties Car Deliveries. Specialist car delivery company.

145 James Traill; Ophthalmic Optician; 1940 to 1976.
Earlier at unnumbered; 1937 to 1938.
Now Forrest Optometrists. Lucy Forrest worked for Malcolm Smith before taking over the practice in 2004 when he retired.

147 Earlier 8 The Broadway
Frank Foster Glanville; Chemist; 1934 to 1951.
S.F Dennis; Dispensing & Photographic Chemist; 1953 to 1962.
M.F Eastwood; Chemist; 1964 to 1976.
Now Pet Doctors, Veterinary Clinic

149 Earlier 7 The Broadway
Dashwood & Sons; Funeral Directors; 1934 to 1964.
Now Hairworld.

151 Earlier 6 The Broadway
Broadway Hairdressing Salon (John Cooper); Ladies' Hairdresser; 1934 to 1940.
Broadway Hairdressing Salon (Miss W Cooper); Ladies' Hairdresser; 1946 to 1964.
Miss W Cooper; Ladies' Hairdresser; 1966.
National Provincial Bank Ltd; 1953 to 1976. Now Fortune House; Chinese Takeaway.

153 Earlier 5 The Broadway

Chapman's Laundry; Receiving Office; 1934 to 1976.
Now Diamond Nails.

The Broadway, Havant Road

155 Earlier 4 The Broadway
Now Evans-Weir; Accountants

157 Earlier 3 The Broaway
George Sheppard or George Sheppard & Sons; Fruiterers; 1934 to 1938.
Albert Edwards; Fruiterer; 1940 to 1960.
L.J West; Fruiterer & Greengrocer; 1964.
Toy & Moore; Fruiterers; 1966 to 1976.
Now KD Physiotherapy. Kevin Dunleavy also at Cams Hall, Fareham.

159 Earlier 2 The Broadway
A confectioners for many years with William Mortimer; Confectioner; 1934 to 1940. Then Mrs Elsie Mortimer; Confectioner; 1946 to 1956.
Mrs M.F Browne; Confectioner; 1958 to 1962.
Remained a confectioners until 1976.

Now Ocean City Recruitment.

161 Earlier 1 The Broadway
A fishmonger from 1934 to 1971 with Albert Francis; 1948 to 1967.
Later became a fish and chip shop with Drayton Fisheries; 1973 to 1976.
Now Drayton Fish & Chips.

On the corner of Drayton Lane is a large stone - Borough of Portsmouth 1920, Mayor John Timpson. This marks the extension of the Borough which enabled 1,500 houses to be built on the hillslopes, in what could be described as the Welsh Estate; and to the south in the Scottish Estate.

here is Drayton Lane

New Inn; 1936 to 1976
A 19th century building with Victorian glass canopy. In 1953 Brickwood & Co Ltd made internal alterations to the pub. Now an Indian Restaurant, Spice Village.

> "The first blacksmith using this site was John Duffin, who lived in an adjoining dwelling house called 'Barkshire Garden', He inherited the land from his mother, Mary Duffin, in 1703. Stables, a barn and an orchard were subsequently added. The Smithy is shown on a map dated 1897, so presumably it was used for blacksmithing up to at least this date. The present building is used as a garage and store by the landlord of the New Inn.
> The present building was constructed by Henry Bransbury in 1839 on the site of the Brewhouse which originally stood there. The first inn dating back to 1750, was a coaching inn with stables and outhouses serving persons travelling along the Turnpike Road from Portsmouth to Chichester. The Royal Mail between Portsmouth and Chichester used to travel by horse drawn coaches along this road. There were still people connected with Farlington who could remember this coach as it passed St Andrews Church about 9 o'clock at night, up to about 1914."
>
> Sylvia Webb

167-173
Was planned to be Drayton Library in 1968.

175-177

Futcher School of Recovery; 1936 to 1967.
The school has its origins in November 1925 when Mr T .W Futcher offered as a free gift the property known as Drayton Lodge and the estate in its entirety consisting of 3 acres of ground, the lodge and five cottages; for use in connection with crippled and delicate children of the Borough. This was organised by a small committee chaired by J.T Rowland. The only reservation made was that should at any time the estate should not be used for the stated purpose that it shall revert to the committee. In 1926 the lodge was to altered and equipped for £3,000. However by September tenders were invited for the erection of a school for which Humphreys Ltd, tender of £1,999 was accepted with the tender of £1,084 for foundations, drainage, heating & lighting from E & A Sprigings accepted. In 2003 the City Council decided to close the school and sell the land for development, merging the school with East Shore School and build a new school in Locksway Road, Milton. The charity commissioners gave permission provided that the proceeds from the sale go towards the new school. Mr Futcher's great-great niece wanted the name to be transferred to the new school. However, when it opened it was named the Mary Rose Academy, still catering for pupils with special needs.

So who was Thomas Futcher - Thomas William Futcher was born in 1852 at Fovant in Wiltshire, the son of a farmer James Futcher. He seems to have been in banking all his working life. In 1871 he is listed as a bank clerk, but only as a visitor to a farm in Hammoon, Dorset. In 1891 he is lodging at Newcastle Upon Tyne as a bank accountant. In 1893 he married Rosa Jeffery at St Edmunds, Salisbury when he is listed as bank manager at Hull. In 1901 he was at Hunslet, West Yorkshire as a bank manager, with his wife and 2 servants and in1911 as a bank manager aged 58, living at Drayton Lodge with his wife Rosa, 49, and two servants.
The Hampshire Telegraph of 27th June 1919 reports that "For 16 years Mr T.W Futcher has been a genial personality in business circles in his capacity as manager of the Commercial Road branch of the National Provincial Bank, and his impending retirement, after 52 years continuous service with the firm, will occasion general regret. Born in Wiltshire in 1852, and comes from an old farming family. At an early age he went to live with his uncle, a sucessful, Dorsetshire farmer. His first appointment in 1867 was at Sturminster Newton, He subsequently held appointments at Leicester, Peterborough, Lichfield,

Hanley, Sunderland, Hull, Leeds and Portsmouth. His first managerial position was at Hull where he opened a new branch. His hobby was rearing of poultry and pigeons. His house at Drayton is filled with awards for his exhibits in the great shows."

Later in the 25th May 1928 issue his obituary reads "It is with great regret that we record the death of Mr Thomas William Futcher, whose kindness and generosity about two years and a half ago made it possible for Portsmouth to have an open air school on the southern slope of Portsdown Hill at Drayton. Mr and Mrs Futcher moved from Drayton Lodge when they handed their late residence over to the trustees for use in the interests of crippled children, and they have since resided at Kent Lodge, Seafield Road, Southborne near Bournemouth, where Mr Futcher passed away on Monday after a short illness, at the advance age of 75 years. His long and close association with the affairs of Portsmouth and his intense interest in its welfare, and especially the welfare of its children, prompted him to take the philanthropic action that resulted in the establishment at Drayton Lodge of the Futcher Council School of Recovery. It was in the autumn of 1925 that Mr Futcher was approached with reference to the use of Drayton Lodge for the benefit of Portsmouth children, and he named a sum which was so exceedingly moderate that it was quickly raised, and the estate of three acres, with its house, lawns and gardens, were acquired and handed over to the local Education Committee free of cost. It is, of course, well known that an open air school was erected in a meadow and that since last summer a fine piece of work has been going on in the way of giving educational facilities and convalescent treatment to about 60 children who are crippled or too delicate to take advantage of ordinary elementary education. The funeral took place at Boscombe Cemetery yesterday."

The Evening News on 10th Feb 1940 has a short item by William Gates "If the spirit of Thomas Futcher ever re-visits his former home ... he must have been thrilled when the children now cared for there, handed over nineteen hundred farthings to provide breakfasts for the poorest little boys and girls of Portsea. Not only the value of the gift, but the spirit that prompted it. How well I remember the day when I formed one of a small party, including Sir John Rowland and Mr W Tomkinson, which by invitation, visited him at his beautiful home at Drayton and, over a cup of tea, listened to this 'Look here, you fellows, if you can secure for me and my wife a modest annuity, I will transfer to you this house and grounds, with the adjoining cottages,

upon your undertaking to make use of the same for the benefit of delicate children,' Needless to say we all felt a throb at the heart as we accepted this splendid gift, and today the Futcher School of Recovery is a priceless memorial."
Langstone Court flats were built in Drayton Lane and Havant Road on the site of the school, planning application 2006.

In the grass verge nearby can be seen an old milestone with the mileage to Havant and Portsmouth.

183 F Partington, Physician & Surgeon; 1960 to 1967. Still listed 1971 to 1976 but not as surgery.
187 Converted into Abbeyfield Home, planning application 1989.
191 The Haven Rest Home, the change to rest home started with 2 ground floor flats being converted in 1971, followed in 1982 by a first floor flat
197 Hillside, Ronald Victor Kenroy, Dental Surgeon; 1936 to 1967.
199-201
Kinross Care Home. Started at 199 with planning application in 1988, later in the year, 201 was added to the home.

here are Portsdown Avenue and Farlington Avenue

South Side

here is Tregaron Avenue

East Court an older villa shown in the directories from 1830. Later from 1923 to 1958 David Gammans who built many houses in the area lived here.

146-156
East Court Nursing Home (Cosham) Ltd; Medical & Convalescent Home; 1960 to 1976. However, the planning application for conversion from private house to nursing home at 156 was in 1968. 158 was added in 1981, 160 in 1985.
156-160 are now Nightingale Court, 36 retirement/sheltered accommodation, flats built in 2002 by McCarthy & Stone.

here is Carshalton Avenue

184-190
Houses built in 1966 on site of nursery gardens, in Havant Road and Lordington Close.

192 E & F Motors Ltd; Motor Engineers; 1960 to 1962.
Later Broadway Garage; Motor Engineers; 1964 to 1966: Wadhams Ltd; Motor Engineers; 1967: Express Garage Ltd (Portsea Island Co-op Society Ltd); 1971 to 1976: Pooles (Cosham) Ltd; Motor Agents; 1976.
Now Co-op grocery store, moving here from the opposite side of the road.

194 Medlam & Co; Surveyors, Auctioneers & Estate Agents; 1956 to 1973.
Later Medlam, Son & Trippick; Estate Agents; 1975 to 1976.
Now In2Kitchens with Drayton Precision Dental above at 194a.

196 F.W Fleming; Confectioner; 1958 to 1971.
"Flemings was almost opposite the New Inn. Friends at school had told me, my friend Ellen Betteridge and others that there were vacancies for paperboys and girls at the shop. We obtained a youth employment card and joined. Pat Russell, Marilyn, Valerie and others also joined or were already there. Our first outing was with Pete Hadley. The Portsdown round and I had a slight accident on my bike skidding at a bend. When later I did the round because someone was ill I was very reticent to go into a corner house in Portsdown Road because of an Alsatian, the postman volunteered to put the paper in for me. I didn't have a regular round during the week I made up the rounds in the morning, counted out News in the evening and either helped with rounds or did Mrs Flemings' shopping usually only bits and pieces and cat's fish half price with old newspapers at the fishmonger at No 1 and frozen peas from the Coop. The Sunday round I did was started by going up Drayton Lane which is beside the New Inn. Roger Hardingham did the Camarthen round and asked for help

when we got to the road. He had two other females helping. Number 45 Camarthen had her shopping done by him bits and pieces again and he always got a big tip at Christmas. An Alsatian dog lived there.
Ellen did Central Round on the flat but had 80 odd News to deliver in the evening the round was started by going down Laburnum Road. When I did her round in the morning and evening I was warned about a dog in a bungalow in Holmleigh Road. Don't put your fingers anywhere near the letter box he'll have them. In the evening there were quite a few people in the garden including a little boy who told me that his dog was very friendly, he almost jumped over the gate at me.
There was a paper strike at the time I was at the paper shop next door to the new Co-op. We would arrive at the shop just before 7 o'clock and the papers would be outside tied up in string. Mr Fleming would give everybody a hack cough lozenge in the winter. He was a handsome man with dark hair a little rotund and smoked a lot, his wife, Florence Louisa (known as Jane) was considered a bit of a dragon. His son in law and daughter ran the other Flemings' along the road.
Pat Russell did the Carshalton Round this started with the nursery which would have been next door the now Co-op Store, we delivered to the bungalow behind. Later my Aunt Jane Florence Louisa and Uncle Fred Cousins; Ann, Lyn and Paul Gunter all lived here. The approach was down Lower Drayton Lane turn right into Racton Road and turn right into Lordington Road. Fred worked for Havant County Council in the Planning Office and was responsible for the Havant Bypass which we called Fred's road. My Aunt died a few years after moving into the house. Fred always liked his gardening and it was because it was possibly part of the former nursery or surrounds it was a success. Greenhouse and vegetables and gourds. Fred played darts at the New Inn and dad would often join him in a round."

Sylvia Webb

Like Sylvia, her brother Frank worked for Flemings

"I had the Carmarthen Round. It was an uphill delivery including over 40 Telegraphs, 15 Expresses and 15 Daily Mails. There were also The Times, Financial Times along with other titles such as the Daily Herald, the Sketch and Daily Worker which have long gone. It was nice to reach the top of the road, cycle along Portsdown Hill until the top of the next road and then it was downhill to complete the round."

Frank Thompson

Now Jefferies Estate Agents.

198 A.F Payne; Wallpaper Merchant; 1960.
Earlier E Figgins & Sons; Decorators' Merchants; 1958.
Later Payne's; Electrical Goods Dealers; 1962 to 1967: Payne's Hardware Stores; 1971 to 1976.
Now BETFRED.

200 Brunswick Family Laundry Co Ltd & Brunswick Dyeing & Cleaning Co Ltd; 1960 to 1964.
Now Drayton Barber Shop.

202-214
Terrace of shops with flats above.

202 A.T Hember; Hairdresser; 1958 to 1976.
Now The Loft Conversion Company, established in 1994.

204-206
Mrs W Baker; Café; 1958 to 1962.
Earlier Mrs W Baker; Café, 206 only; 1953 to 1956.
Later K.R McInnes; Café; 1964: W Carter; Café; 1966 to 1967: Windmill Café; 1973 to 1975.
Now Take Away Food Centre; Chinese, 1976 to 2017.

208 S.T Slape; Fishmonger; 1946 to 1976.
Earlier C.E Slape; Fishmonger; 1940.
Now Kentucky Fried Chicken.

210 A Post Office and newsagent from 1946 to 1976 with Mrs K.W Dolbear; Stationer & Post Office; 1960 to 1964.
Earlier Henry E Brown; Post Office; 1946 to 1953: Mrs K.W Brown; Post Office; 1956 to 1958.
Now Drayton Models.

212 Maison Drayton (S.W Smith); Ladies' Hairdresser; 1948 to 1962.
Earlier Maison Drayton; Ladies' Hairdressers; 1938 to 1940: S.W Smith; Hairdresser; 1946.
Later Maison Drayton (Mrs R.K Smith); Ladies' Hairdresser; 1964 to 1966: Maison Drayton (Mrs K Privett); Ladies' Hairdresser; 1967: Maison Drayton (Mrs K Privett & Mrs R.K Smith); Ladies' Hairdresser; 1971 to 1976.
Still Maison Drayton, Ladies' Hairdressers in 2017.
The family business was founded by Samuel Whitmore Smith in 1945, taking over the earlier hairdressers. The business remained in the family with his daughter Kathleen Privett. Closed in March 2017 on retirement of Kathleen, at the age of 93, who was assisted by her daughter and daughter-in-law.

Now G & Co, Hair Dressing
214 Campions (Bakers) Ltd; 1956 to 1964.
Heath Café in 2017

here is Lower Drayton Lane

Earlier Wellington Terrace, 1-5; 1953 to 1958 and Wellington Cottage; 1953 to 1956, were here.

Brewers Sales & Letting Agents opened a small office here converting the former public convenience on the corner.

224a-e Planning permission for the shops and maisonettes was raised in 1959. The shops are listed from 1962.

224a Joly & Bradburn Ltd, Photographers & Chemists; 1962 to 1967.
Now BHI Building Services

224b Weston's Bakers; 1962. F Wilkins (1930) Ltd, Bakers, 1964 to 1976. (The same company)
Now Blossoms, Florist. Opened in 2013.

224c Jarrett's, Shoe Dealers; 1962 to 1971. Gaytons, Shoe Retailers, 1973 to 1976.
Now Drayton News.

224d E.W.N Electrics Ltd, Electrical Appliances; 1962 to 1964. Later R.A Fraser (Drayton) Ltd, Electrical Appliances, 1966 to 1976.
Now Sue Ryder, Charity Shop

224e Broadway Confections; 1962 to 1967.
Now Rowans Hospice, Charity Shop

224f G Cooper, Butcher; 1962 to 1976.
Now TLC Hair Studio, established in 1997.

224g H Wain & Sons Ltd, Grocers/Fruiterers; 1962 to 1967. Still a fruiterer 1971 to 1973, Quartons.
Now Cameo Brides of Drayton, founded in 1989.

226 Bowmakers, Bankers, 1971 to 1976.

228 Smith & Vosper Ltd; 1936 to 1938, then again from 1951 to 1960.
Now Hampshire Face & Laser Clinic

Squeezed into the space between 228 and 230 is the Snack Shack.

230-232 W Pink & Sons; 1938 to 1975. Still a grocers, Moores; in 1976.
Earlier listed from 1936 to 1937 as Drayton House. From 2013 to 2017 The Red Lounge, restaurant which closed in June 2017. Now reopened as Zayns, Bangladeshi Cuisine restaurant, still part of the Red Lounge Group.

Earlier Fay & Sons (E.H Thorn), Drayton Nursery was here; 1951 to 1953. Earlier still S Fay & Sons; 1936 to 1948.

here is Aldworth Path

234 Listed as tobacconist/newsagent/confectioner over the years from 1936 to 1976 with F.W Fleming, 1948 to 1966. Now Stage 2, Hair Studio.

236 Off Licence from 1938 to 1976 with Geo Peters & Co Ltd, W & S; 1938 to 1960. Now Straight to the Point, Tattoo Studio.

238 Drayton Institute; 1936 to 2017.
Founded in 1920. The institute was built as a memorial to the men of Drayton who were killed in the First World War. Now known as The Drayton Centre.

240 Butchers from 1936 to 1976 with J Ford, only listed in 1960. Now Drayton Coffee House.

242 Newsagents from 1938 to 1976 with E & I Bryant; 1960 to 1967. From 1938 to 1946 was listed as Stanley Alder, earlier his shop is shown at what was later 258; 1936 to 1937. Later Mrs Alder, Newsagent; 1948 to 1956.

"My uncle Stanley was in World War 1, he was in the Royal Army Medical Corps. Sadly his brother Sidney came back from the war and committed suicide. Stanley married Nelly Moody, they lived at 242 Havant Road. He had a sweet shop, he died in 1940 leaving money to another brother Walter Joseph Alder."

Susannah Kimber

244 Confectioner from 1936 to 1976 with William Jarman, 1936 to 1946. W.J Jarman (W.G & D Keys), Confectioners; 1948 to 1964, then Jarman; 1966 to 1976.
242-244 now Emsworth Aquaria & Reptiles. Moved here from North Street, Emsworth.

246 Chemist from 1936 to 1976 with J.H.G Stuart, Chemist; 1948 to 1966. Now Drayton Cycles.

248-250
Drapers from 1936 to 1962 with Gosling (Cosham) Ltd, Drapers; 1958 to 1962.
248 now Drayton Stores
250 now Alexandra Gray Interiors, Chandeliers & Mirrors.

252 Butchers from to 1936 to 1960 with V.A Street, Butcher; 1948 to 1960. Later D.M Street, Drayton (Motor Cycle) Accessories; 1962 to 1964. Now Meridian Funeral Services, part of the Co-op group.

254 Barclays Bank Ltd; 1953 to 1967. Now Emberz, Stoves & Fireplaces

256 Bakers from 1948 to 1976. G.W Green Ltd, Bakers; 1956 to 1960. Later Smith & Vosper Ltd; 1962 to 1976. Now a branch of Heidi's Pattiserie.

258 Drayton Fruit Shop (J.B Mugford); 1940 to 1962. Now HCM, Home & Commercial Mortgages Ltd

260-262

Smith & Son, Boot Dealers; 1936 to 1967.
Now Workshop Recruitment.

264a Joykay (Drayton) Ltd, Wool Stores; 1960 to 1976. Now Wonderful Nails.

264b T.S Jones, Watchmaker; 1960 to 1976. Now Drayton Community Chemist.

264 J.V Figgins (Builders) Ltd; 1960 - at the rear.

264c Now Best Pals Cosham Dog Grooming

264e Lancaster (John) Radiators Ltd, Motor Radiator Repairs; 1960 at the rear of 264.

266 Nappers, Builders' Merchants; 1960 to 1967. They are listed as Decorators in 1951 to 1958.
Rebuilt as Phoenix House. Drayton Sweet Jar was here from 2010 to 2017 when it closed. Now the Drayton branch of Enthuse Care, care agency.

268 Hyman Levy. He is listed here from 1936 to 1971 although only as a tailor from 1958 to 1960.

270 The Glen Coffee Lounge; 1960 to 1964. Glen Restaurant; 1966 to 1976. Now Mowchak, Tandoori Restaurant, 2011-2017.
Earlier was Miss E Mockford , Wool Stores; 1958.
"At the top of Laburnum Avenue was an orchard and the first house past that turning left was Miss Mugford. (this could be a memory lapse as Mugford were at 258 and this is Mockford) You went down her drive at the side and her front door was always open. You couldn't enter but stod on the doorstep and there were shelves up to the ceiling with skeins of wool of every colour . She must have been in her late fifties with grey hair and a bun. She was quite short, but she knew where everything was and would climb ladders to reach the top. I was always there buying wool for my aunt, I would then sit arms outstretched while she wound it into balls."
Jean Ridgeon

272 Russell Wicks, Shopkeeper; 1958 to 1960. Later Laburnum Stores, Grocers; 1962 to 1976. Now Grace Court, planning application

raised in 2005, architects Ken Scadden Associates.

here is footpath to Laburnum Avenue

274-276

A planning application was raised for for two houses, with verandahs and garages in 1953 by W.H Hellier Ltd. Doctors surgery from 1956 to 1976 with William George Cheyne, Victor Martindale, Treffy John Thompson & F.J O'Connell, Physicians & Surgeons; 1960 to 1967. Now Rowlands Pharmacy.

280 Now The Drayton Surgery. 278-280 were demolished and the new health centre planned in 1995, modified in 1999 and 2007.

Drayton Methodist Church, now combined with Cosham United Reformed Church and known as Drayton United Church. Listed from 1936.

Drayton United Church, Havnt Road

R Bray in his Drayton Trial refers to the original church of 1916 which is probably the building at the rear of the new church and the west of the newer halls. It has foundation stones incorporated in the northern wall which may have been relocated. Mrs W.J Avens on behalf of Wesley Institute; Mrs George Taylor; A.S Juniper, New Barnet; The Ladies of Drayton; Mr J Wilson, Superintendent on behalf of Wesley Sunday School; Miss Edna Marie Vine; Miss R Gauntlett; Miss Evelyn Wyatt in memory of Hugh Wyatt Esq, JP of Lincoln.

The foundation stones of the newer church are on the north side by the entrance and are plain.

The foundation stone of the new hall was laid by the Right Worshipful Lord

Mayor of Portsmouth Alderman Albert Johnson JP 28th June 1952; Commemorating the gift of Twyford Avenue Trust by Rev George Standing CBE, DSO, MC.
A further hall was added in 1976.

Laburnum Avenue

"I was born in Laburnum Avenue in Drayton in May 1944, 11 days before D-Day. The bungalow where I was born belonged to my grandparents James and Ellen Fordham and was built by my uncle. I believe he bought a piece of land that belonged to the railway. Laburnum Avenue was lined with Laburnum trees which were covered with yellow blossom all through May, they looked a picture. These have all been cut down because of the fear of poisoning from the flowers.

My mother Doris Fordham, then Rogers, who is now 92 (2016), was an ambulance driver at the ARP Post at Futchers School. Mum is only four foot eleven inches tall and she drove a Wessex Terraplane ambulance. It was navy blue with a red cross and was kept in use up to the 1950s. I remember her pointing it out to me as a child, when the ambulances were parked at the gateway to St Mary's Hospital. She said they put wooden blocks on the pedals so she could reach them. She was 17, and her sister Mary was 19, they lived at Purbrook and would walk down Drayton Lane in the blackout to come on duty at Drayton. Many times they would be halfway up the lane, walking home and there would be a red alert and they would have to rush back. She has memories of popping into the Drayton Institute while she was on duty for a quick dance, during the afternoon, when a tea dance was on and running back across the road before she was missed!

My father's parents lived in Drayton and grandad, James Fordham, was a submariner from the First World War. He was partly paralysed and had Parkinson's disease which gave his hand a continual shake. He drove a petrol invalid chair and would pester all the Drayton shopkeepers by sitting outside and whistling until they came out to serve him. He was well known in Drayton because he used to sit outside the chip shop selling poppies for the British Legion. He had a chow dog called Bruin who used to sit under his invalid chair. One day another dog came along and they both started to fight under grandad's chair and tipped him out, poppies flew everywhere and passers by had to stop and haul the chair and grandad back to rights. He was also well known in the New Inn private bar, where he would

drink his half of bitter. I used to go in the bottle and jug with a screw top bottle for bitter, I must have been about 9 at the time!
You could buy anything in Drayton at that time. In the late forties and early fifties the range of shops were so different. Now Drayton is full of takeaways. In those days there was a shoe shop, 2 wet fish shops, 2 greengrocers, 2 bakers, 3 butchers. There was also a large grocery store, Pinks, where the Red Lounge now stands. I remember buying sugar in there loose, scooped out of a large drum and put into a blue paper cornet.
We knew all the names of the shopkeepers. Mr Marshall was the manager of Pinks, a tall man with a moustache. Mr Wynne kept the toy shop where, the old Co-Op was situated, and my brother Barry bought all his Dinky cars. My dad took him up on Friday (payday) and paid 2/6 for a racing car or tank. They were so well made and heavy. I often see them now on Flog It or Antiques Roadshow and they are worth a fortune. Mr Wynne had a shock of coarse white hair that stood on end. He was a family friend and dad always said his hair became like that after he taught dad to drive! There was also a pram shop, Keasts, on the corner of Drayton Lane where mum bought my pram. The fish and chip shop is still there and behind it in Drayton Lane my uncle Jack Hartley had a car repair workshop. Mr Stuart ran one of the chemists and there were always big coloured bottles in the window.
On the south side of the Havant Road where the antique shop now stands there was a big drapers called Allens. My mum used to buy my baby clothes there, and my liberty bodices with the rubber buttons. Mr Allen was a dapper little man, very similar to Arthur Lowe in looks. There was even an upholsterer, Rushtons, further up the near Lights the hardware store. Rushtons and the toy shop stood on the site of the British Restaurant which was used in the war. My Aunt Nell was cashier there and nicknamed ‘Cash’ forever afterwards. After the war she and her manageress, Miss Jackman, moved on to work at Hilsea Lido.
Next to the New Inn was a row of terraced cottages and the end cottage was used for ARP staff to sleep in. Mum said there was a passage from it to Futcher House. Opposite the New Inn was a piece of waste ground and another row of cottages, Wellington Terrace behind it.
I worked in Maison Drayton the hairdressers in the 1960s and did an apprenticeship. It is still a hairdressers today (2016). In the cellar where we washed the towels there were lots of heat perm machines

where you were strung up with wire and big bottles wrapped in straw. It was fascinating to us apprentices at that time as we thought we were bang up to the minute with beehives and backcombing.

Where Springfield School now stands in Central Road there were allotments. When they were abandoned after the war, us kids would spend hours down there picking blackberries. They were the big cultivated berries. The senior school for the area was Court Lane before Springfield was built, it also had a junior school. The junior school for Drayton was Solent Road and the overflow for the infants was in the Methodist Church hall. My dad, Jim Fordham, went to Solent Road and I took my eleven plus there. All four of my grandchildren have attended Solent Road.

It is a shame to see most of the old shops now gone..."

Jean Ridgeon

In 1952 6 new houses & garages were proposed by N.E Wilson

Lower Drayton Lane

Earlier the road was part of Drayton Lane but the name was changed at the request of the residents to avoid confusion. The southern part near Flint house was diverted in 1955 to provide suitable access to old people's home.

Between what are now Racton Avenue and Southbourne Avenue on the west were the farm buildings of Drayton Farm.

The Drayton Farm estate was developed by D Gammans in 1925.

On the west just south of what is now Dysart Avenue was Drayton Manor. See Dysart Avenue in the first section of this booklet.

Lower Drayton Farm was on the east, south of Old Manor Way and was purchased by the Council Electricity Department in 1946.

In 1952 G Cooper exchanged 41acres of Lower Drayton Farm for industrial and housing use; for 67.7 acres including marsh land. Also an outbuilding converted to bungalow.

"In Lower Drayton Lane where the entrance to roughly where Drayton car park is now were the remains of farm buildings. They were built of brick and flint. A friend and myself had the strange hobby of collecting flint stones with crystals in them (this was in the late 1940s). At the time we were about 8 years old and although a fair distance from out homes, in Highbury, we would often ride there. We enjoyed climbing over piles of rubble and my friend found a broken flint with a lovely gathering of blue crystals in it."

Malcolm Garlick

Pangbourne Avenue

North Side

5 John Folland & Sons; Decorators; 1956 to 1976.

Penarth Avenue

No8 was a new house for P.J Warren 1952.

Penrhyn Avenue

West, East and South sides, residential only.

North Side

here is Merthyr Avenue

Church of the Resurrection; 1930 to 2017.

In 1929 a planning application was raised for a new church by Portsmouth Diocesan Extension Committee.

> "The site was chosen partly because the rector thought it would be away from the sounds of traffic, but we note that the land was cheaper at 5 shilling per square yard than land on Havant Road at 8 shillings. The land was bought from Mr Gammans, iron founder and developer for £1,125. At a meeting in 1928 the diocese agreed to pay for the shell of the church and the parish would need to complete and furnish it. The architect was Mr Randoll Blacking of Paget & Seeley, the builders were Samuel Salter & Co of Portsmouth. The foundation stone was laid on 22nd April 1930 by Lady Heath Harrison of Liss who also gave £1,000 for the organ which was by Ivemy's of Southampton. The church was consecrated on 11th October."
>
> Church of Resurrection web-site

New halls were added to the north-west of the site, foundation stone laid in 1955, by Launcelot (Flemming) Bishop of Portsmouth.

here is Brecon Avenue

Portsdown Avenue

Residential apart from the Carlton Club, a private sports and social club, at 16-18 from 1951 to 1976. Still operating in 2017.

South Road

The was extended in 1935

East Side

Residential only

West Side

here is Central Road

South Road Church

This started as a house fellowship group. The existing main church was built in 1935.

Station Road

Named after Farlington Station/Halt that was at the southern end serving the racecourse.

Numbers 81-83 were new in 1946 as was the Co-op Bakery and Leethams planned a factory here at the junction with Grove Road.

The co-op also built a large dairy here. The Southern Dairy Depot was here until 2007. After many years there are now plans for a new housing estate on the site.